Hudson Taylor

Hudson Taylor

by
Fern Neal Stocker

A Guessing Book

MOODY PRESS
CHICAGO

© 1986 by
THE MOODY BIBLE INSTITUTE
OF CHICAGO

All Scripture quotations are from the King James Version.

Illustrations are by Virginia Hughins.

Library of Congress Cataloging in Publication Data

Stocker, Fern Neal, 1917-
  Hudson Taylor.

  (A Guessing book)
  Summary: Examines the life of the missionary whose
difficult experiences in China tested and proved his
trust in God and led him to start the China Inland
Mission. At intervals in the text the reader finds a
question followed by several possible answers, one or
more of which may be correct.
  1. Taylor, James Hudson, 1832-1905—Juvenile
literature.   2. Missionaries—China—Biography—
Juvenile literature.   3. Missionaries—United States—
Biography—Juvenile literature.   [1. Taylor, James
Hudson, 1832-1905.   2. Missionaries.   3. Literary
recreations]   I. Hughins, Virginia, ill.   II. Title.
III. Series: Stocker, Fern Neal, 1917- . Guessing book.
BV3427.T3S76   1986   266'.0092'4 [B] [92]   86-21731
ISBN 0-8024-8575-8 (pbk.)

1 2 3 4 5 6 7 Printing/LC/Year 91 90 89 88 87 86

Printed in the United States of America.

To Janine Long

Contents

To You, the Reader:

A Guessing Book is the story of a famous person. As you read along in this Guessing Book, you'll come to questions you can answer by yourself.

One, two, or three guesses are given, and you can choose one, two, or three answers. Sometimes all are correct, sometimes none. (You'll find the answer as you keep reading.) Pretty soon you'll know the person in the story so well you can get the answer right every time.

It may be fun to keep track of how many guesses you get right. But if you miss one, don't worry—this isn't a test.

Read this Guessing Book and learn about Hudson Taylor, a man who trusted God no matter what.

1

The Fire Did It

"**B**ut Mother, I don't want to go to bed!" Hudson Taylor was caught up in an exciting part of a story and had no intention of leaving it until it was finished.

"But you must get to bed so that you can go to school in the morning." Mother was firm.

Hudson decided to

| GUESS |

1. go to bed as directed.
2. find a way to sneak a candle to bed.
3. turn on the electric light after she was gone.

Mother always took the candle away after she heard prayers at the Taylor home. But Hudson knew she kept the candle ends in the cellar to be melted and reformed into new candles. He slipped down to the cellar and stuffed his pocket with candle ends. That's how life was in England in 1840.

He planned to

| GUESS |

1. read by the light of the burning candle ends.
2. stick the ends together to make a long candle.
3. chew the wax.

"Hudson Taylor! Why are you bleeding?"

His plan was to burn the candle ends one by one until he finished his story. Before escaping to his bedroom, he entered the study to say good night to his father and a visitor. *I'll make this short,* he promised himself.

"Oh, Hudson, I'm so glad you came in," exclaimed the visitor. "I've been saving a story for you. Come sit on my lap, and I'll tell it to you."

Hudson tried to excuse himself, "But it is late, and Mother has told me to go to bed."

"That's all right, Son," Father interrupted. "Just sit on the footstool beside the fireplace." Father was aware that Hudson considered himself too old for sitting on laps.

Hudson decided to

GUESS	1. object and leave the room.
	2. be polite and sit on the footstool.
	3. sit on the gentleman's lap.

Hudson felt obliged to be polite. He pulled the footstool to the visitor's chair. This put his bulging pocket directly in front of the fire. "What story do you have tonight, Sir?" he asked.

The visitor began his story. Any other time Hudson would have enjoyed it. Tonight, however, he couldn't wait to get upstairs to read his book. *Will he never finish?* Hudson wondered.

"Hudson Taylor! Why are you bleeding?" Mother suddenly screamed as red drops fell to the rug under Hudson.

Hudson was bleeding because

GUESS	1. the heat of the fire was burning him.
	2. he had an old wound that opened.
	3. the red candles in his pocket were melting.

The red candles in his pocket had melted, as his mother soon discovered.

"Hudson, why do you have these candle ends in your pocket?" He tried to think of a lie, but none came to him.

So he

| GUESS |

1. said nothing.
2. told the truth.
3. mumbled something no one could understand.

Hudson couldn't think of anything but the truth, so he told it. *Mother can look at me and see a lie anyhow,* he thought.

After he told what he planned to do with the candle ends, his mother said,

| GUESS |

1. "Go to bed."
2. "Oh, my son, how could you disappoint me so?"
3. "You could have burned the house down!"

While his mother worried about the house burning, Father sent Hudson to bed. Hudson knew he would be punished.

His punishment the next day was

| GUESS |

1. ten lashes with the razor strap.
2. forty strokes with the spanking board.
3. no ice cream for a week.

Hudson received ten lashes with the razor strap. Father said, "This hurts me more than it does you."

Hudson's father was

| GUESS |

1. a druggist
2. strict.
3. a Christian.

James Taylor was a strict Christian druggist in England. He punished Hudson because he loved him and wanted him to be good.

Hudson thought his punishment was too much, since he had

not, in fact, even burned the candle ends.

So he

GUESS

1. went to Grandfather's house.
2. sulked all day.
3. wouldn't speak to Father for a week.

Hudson went to Grandfather Hudson's library. His mother's father was a

GUESS

1. coal miner.
2. preacher.
3. maker of reeds.

Grandfather Taylor was a maker of reeds; Hudson's great-grandfather James Taylor was a coal miner; but Grandfather Hudson was a preacher. Since all were Christians, Hudson had heard Bible stories and preaching all his life.

Hudson was named for

GUESS

1. his father.
2. his father and grandfather.
3. his great-grandfather.

He was named "James" for his father and great-grandfather and "Hudson" for his mother's father. His mother said, "I want people to know who I mean when I say 'James,' so I'll call the boy by his second name." And so he became known as Hudson Taylor.

When Hudson was only five years old, he was asked, "What do you want to be when you grow up?"

He said,

GUESS

1. "A coal miner."
2. "A preacher."
3. "A missionary to China."

15

Hudson wanted to be a missionary to China when he was five. Did he say the same thing when he was twelve years old?

GUESS

1. Yes.
2. No.

No. After he went to school at Barnsley, he wanted to follow the world. He wanted to be important.

Hudson was sickly. He missed so much school that he finally stayed at home and studied with his parents. He also helped his father in the drug store.

His father often invited friends and customers to dinner. Mother never knew how many people were coming. Sometimes she became flustered. One day she served a crowd, and Hudson waited and waited for his plate and silverware. He realized his mother had forgotten him in the excitement, but he was hungry.

So he

GUESS

1. called out loudly for food.
2. asked for the salt.
3. jumped up from the table.

Hudson said, "Please pass the salt so that I will be ready when Mother remembers my plate."

Another time he was left out as the apple pie was passed around. After a long wait, he said,

GUESS

1. "Is apple pie good for boys?"
2. "I am hungry for apple pie."
3. "Please pass some pie, Mother."

Hudson asked if apple pie was good for boys, and he received his portion.

Since Grandfather Hudson was the preacher at Pinefold Hill and the family attended church regularly, Hudson was expected to

16

| GUESS |

1. read the Bible.
2. pray in public.
3. quote Bible verses.

He was expected to pray and quote the Bible in public. That was easy to do because he had heard it at home for twelve years. When he was supposed to be reading, however, he often had something else inside his Bible that interested him more.

His mother was not fooled. She knew Hudson was not a Christian, even though he lived in a Christian home. "Always remember I'm praying for you," she said.

2

Grandmother's Birds

"**H**udson, your grandmother sent word for you and Amelia to come to her house after lunch."
Hudson replied,

GUESS

1. "What does she want, Mother?"
2. "That's strange—Grandmother never calls."
3. "I want to go swimming."

Hudson said, "I want to go swimming."
"I know you had other plans, Son, but you know Grandmother is paralyzed and never calls."
After lunch, Hudson found himself drifting down the path and past the church to Grandmother's house. Seeing his friend Johnny, Hudson called, "Where you going?"
"To Mistress Hudson's home. She sent word she wants me." Johnny looked as surprised as Hudson.
"Do you know why?"
"No, but she has sent for all the children on this street."
"Really? Why?" questioned Hudson. "I thought Amelia and I were the only ones."
"Let's run. We can be the first there," proposed Johnny.

They weren't first, however. Several curious children were standing outside the gate when Hudson and Johnny arrived.

"Why don't you go in?" questioned Hudson.

"We were waiting for you or Amelia. She's your grandmother. What does she want?"

"I don't know," Hudson had to admit. "But come on. I know how to unlock the gate. We will have to walk in because Grandmother can't get out of her bed to open the door."

The crowd of children stood quietly while Hudson opened the door. As he wiped his feet, they did likewise, before crossing the carpet in the parlor. Amelia and her friend Josie joined them as they walked quietly into the clean, white bedroom.

"Welcome!" Grandmother beamed. "I see you answered my call for help! As you know, I can't move from this bed because of my old back."

The children nodded, noticing the small lump she made under the spotless white coverlet. Her white face and hair completed the picture. Only her black eyes blazed.

"A month ago the carpenter delivered three birdhouses, a birdbath, and a feeder. They have been sitting in the shed all this time. The Reverend says he will put them up when he gets around to it."

Grandmother paused for breath. "I decided to put them up today while he is gone. I need your help."

"I saw my first robin the other day," Amelia offered. "You are right about its being time to get them up. Let's all get to work!"

"Wait a minute," Grandmother called. "First we have to get organized."

"Who will go to the shed?"

"Who will collect supplies?"

"Who will climb the trees and place the ropes?"

"Who will pull the ropes to raise the birdhouses?"

As the questions were asked, children raised their hands to volunteer, and soon everyone knew what to do.

In no time, the children were chattering, calling directions to each other, and putting up the birdhouses outside the oversized window in Grandmother's room. There were a few close calls.

| GUESS | 1. Hudson almost fell out of the tree. |
| | 2. Susie skinned her knee. |

3. Amelia hit her head on the feeder.

Amelia hit her head.

"I never saw birdhouses tied to a tree with ropes before," Johnny observed.

Grandmother didn't miss that. "Johnny, this is women's carpentry. I won't have you children hammering nails into the apple trees. Tie 'em tight, and the birds'll know no difference."

When they finished placing the birdhouses, they rolled the base for the birdbath in front of the window and carefully set the china bowl of water on top. Then they filled the feeders with birdseed. One of the older girls went into the house and returned with lemonade and little cakes.

As the children ate, Grandmother smiled through the window, waved her thanks, and threw kisses with her good hand.

"Makes you feel good to help out, doesn't it, Red?" Johnny stated what they all felt.

"Don't call me Red!" Hudson objected. His mother greatly admired his beautiful red hair, but Hudson hated it.

As Hudson walked home, he wondered, *Did the children or Grandmother put up the birdhouses? How could Grandmother do anything?*

| GUESS |

1. *She couldn't move.*
2. *She asked for help.*
3. *She organized everything.*

All of that was true.

A week later Hudson sneaked back to observe the birds splashing in the water, going in and out of the houses with straw in their bills, and taking turns feasting on seeds. He slipped to the bedroom window and waved to grandmother lying helpless inside.

Hudson did not know that years later God would use that happening to change his life.

3

It Is Finished

"**A**ren't you a little young to be a clerk in a bank?" asked Alex, the oldest junior clerk.

"I'm fifteen!" defended Hudson. "And I passed the math test like everyone else working here."

"That's funny; they don't even teach some of that math until the last years at school."

"Well, I learned at home. They pushed me as fast as I could learn," explained Hudson.

"Who? Your tutor?"

"No, my mother and father. My father is a druggist."

"Oh, I say, you're James Taylor's son. I know him. He gave me medicine for my gout. Well, welcome to Barnsley Shire Bank." Alex smiled.

Hudson answered,

1. "Oh, you only welcome me because of my father."

GUESS

2. "My parents are better teachers than those at school."

3. "I'm only fifteen, but I'm as smart as you."

Hudson said nothing. He only smiled back at Alex and shook hands. He wanted to be friends with the older boy.

Later that evening Hudson added up the money in his drawer. It was a few pennies more than what his figures showed.

Hudson decided to

GUESS

1. ask Alex what to do.
2. count the money over again.
3. change the numbers already recorded.

Hudson asked Alex what to do.

"Oh, count it over again. If it still comes out more than your record, change the record."

"But is that honest?" objected Hudson.

"Who cares? If you don't do that, you can count half the night until you finally find your error. Who wants to stay here? They don't pay you after five, you know."

Hudson

GUESS

1. did as Alex said.
2. stayed late and found his mistake.
3. put the extra money in his pocket.

Hudson followed Alex's advice.

"Come with the boys to the pub," invited Alex, as they were leaving the bank. "You need a drink after thinking so hard all day."

Hudson said,

GUESS

1. "Not tonight. I promised my sister I'd meet her at five thirty."
2. "Don't you know my grandfather is a preacher? I can't be seen at the pub."
3. "Mama wouldn't want me to go."

It was a struggle to know what to say. He couldn't disgrace

Grandfather or hurt his mother, but he wanted to be friends with the other workers. He was glad he had promised Amelia to go skating. He used that as an excuse.

On the way home, he thought,

GUESS

1. *I'll have to think of a lot of excuses.*
2. *The fellows will get wise to me.*
3. *I wish our family wasn't so religious. I could do what I want.*

Hudson worried about the fellows' opinion of him.

The next day his boss, Mr. Hamilton, called Hudson into the manager's office.

"Last night I stayed late and checked your work for the day. All in all, you did a good job. I wonder, however, why you erased the correct answer to your money receipts and changed it. I could see the numbers you changed under the new numbers. Why did you do this?"

Hudson answered Mr. Hamilton,

GUESS

1. "Because Alex told me to."
2. "Because it didn't agree with the money in my drawer."
3. "It's none of your business."

He said, "Sir, the money in the draw was more than the money shown on the receipts."

"So you changed the record to agree with the facts."

"Exactly, Sir."

"Didn't you know that was dishonest? One reason I hired you was because of your family's reputation for honesty."

Hudson defended himself by saying,

GUESS

1. "I thought it was wrong."
2. "Alex said that was the way to do it."
3. "It seemed all right to me."

25

"Why did you do this?"

"I did think it was wrong," Hudson admitted, "but it was closing time, and I didn't want to take time to find my mistake."

"Young man, let me tell you, you are responsible for your errors. Everyone makes them, but when you are dealing with other people's money, you have to be accurate. Staying late to find your mistakes is the best way to teach you to be careful while working. Never let this happen again! Promise?"

"I promise," Hudson agreed, glad to flee the office.

He didn't have to hunt for an excuse not to go to the pub after that. He was busy adding and re-adding his figures.

He said,

GUESS

1. "The correct answer is here. I just have to find it."
2. "I wish I had an adding machine."
3. "A computer could have kept this all straight."

Hudson re-did his arithmetic until he found his error and corrected it. Sometimes it was midnight when he got home.

During the day, he listened to the older boys chatter about their dates and their drunken sprees and heard them use the Lord's name carelessly.

At first he

GUESS

1. disapproved of what they did.
2. was shocked at their deeds.
3. thought swearing sounded horrible.

Hudson did shudder when he first heard the name of Jesus used as swearing, but he was surprised how soon he became used to it. One day he shocked himself by

GUESS

1. swearing under his breath.
2. swearing in his mind.
3. swearing out loud.

Hudson never swore out loud, but he did swear in his mind. He felt it was wrong

GUESS
1. but not as bad as saying the words.
2. but not like actually hurting someone.
3. but he couldn't help himself.

Hudson had listened to Grandfather's sermons and knew there was really no excuse for swearing, but he wondered if thinking a swear word was actually swearing.
Hudson worked at the bank

GUESS
1. six months.
2. one year.
3. ten years.

Hudson worked at the bank only six months, because

GUESS
1. he couldn't stand the wicked ways of the young men.
2. he had trouble with his eyesight.
3. he became ill.

Hudson had trouble with his eyes because of the close work and the endless checking he did by candlelight after the bank closed.
At home, he missed his job. He couldn't study because of his eyes, and he felt restless and unhappy.
He kept thinking of the boys at the bank. He remembered

GUESS
1. their jokes.
2. their laughter.
3. the fun they told about.

Hudson remembered their laughing as they told jokes and all

28

about their wicked fun. It seemed to him that

GUESS

1. wicked boys had more fun than Christians.
2. wickedness was evil.
3. sin sounded good.

Sin began to sound good to Hudson. It seemed fun to be bad. Going to church and praying all the time seemed

GUESS

1. wonderful.
2. the thing to do.
3. tiresome.

As Hudson's eyes slowly recovered, church seemed tiresome and long. His mother and sister were concerned about him. They

GUESS

1. scolded him.
2. forced him to listen to long Bible passages.
3. prayed for him.

All they did was pray—continually, silently, and fervently.
One day they went to a ladies' meeting eighty miles away. They took the horse and carriage and stayed overnight.
Father went to work, and Hudson was home alone. His eyes were better, so he decided to

GUESS

1. watch television.
2. listen to the radio.
3. read.

Since there was nothing else to do, he decided to read. He picked up one of the booklets on the library table. Seeing it was a religious booklet, he said, "There will be a story at the beginning and a sermon at the end.

29

| GUESS |
1. I'll read the first and leave the rest."
2. The stories are usually good."
3. The sermons are dry."

He decided to read the story and skip the sermon. The story made him think of his father, who was satisfied and happy with the Christian life. "If I could be happy being a Christian, if I could find joy and fun living that way, I'd like it." He read about the finished work of Christ. He realized, "It *is* finished! Christ did it all. Why am I wondering what I can do to be satisfied? I don't have to do anything. Jesus took all my sin on Himself. I don't have to work for salvation. He finished the work on the cross."

Slowly Hudson sank to his knees. "Jesus, I've said prayers before, but now I want to talk to You. I want to tell You I believe You died for me and rose again for me. Thank You for coming to me today."

Hudson was saved because

| GUESS |
1. he prayed.
2. he believed.
3. he worked.

Hudson believed in the Lord Jesus Christ.
The Bible says that if you believe on the Lord Jesus Christ

| GUESS |
1. you will be saved.
2. you can start working.
3. you might get to heaven.

The Bible says, "Believe on the Lord Jesus Christ, and [you will] be saved."

Late that evening Mother and Amelia returned in the carriage. Mother was so excited that she left the horse in the driveway and rushed into the house.

"Hudson, Hudson!" she called. "I was praying this afternoon and God showed me

| GUESS |

1. that you will be a great missionary."
2. that you trusted Christ."
3. that you are to be knighted by the king."

"Mother," called Hudson, "I have something to tell you. I'm a Christian. I believed this afternoon."

"Yes, I know," answered Mother. "That's what God showed me this afternoon."

Mother knew this was the beginning of a great life for Hudson. What she didn't know was that Hudson would never be *her boy* again. Hudson Taylor was now *God's man.*

4

Tests

"How are your eyes, Red?" Grandfather Hudson, the pastor of Pinehill Church, inquired as Hudson shook hands with him.

Hudson was last to leave the church after the service because

GUESS
1. he was hiding.
2. he didn't want anyone to hear Grandfather call him "Red."
3. he wanted to talk to Grandfather.

Hudson had stopped everyone from calling him "Red" except Grandfather.

"My eyes seem good as new," Hudson admitted.

"That's strange. They were so painful a few weeks ago."

"They really did hurt while I worked in the bank. Except for the dreadful pain, I

GUESS
1. would have worked in the bank all my life."
2. would not have been saved."
3. would have played football."

Hudson had enjoyed his job. Now as Grandfather locked the church door, he sensed that Hudson wanted to talk to him. "And what are your plans?" asked Grandfather. "You know that out of suffering come God's greatest warriors.' "

As they walked the few blocks down the dusty road to Grandfather's home, Hudson told his secret.

"When I was praying, I told God I loved Him; I'd do anything for him; I'd follow Him. And do you know what happened?"

"What?" asked Grandfather.

"God seemed to speak to me in the silence. He said, 'Then go for Me to China.' "

"In words you could hear?"

"No," Hudson answered, "not with my ears but in my heart. It was as real as if He spoke out loud."

"What of your parents?" reminded Grandfather.

"Father wants me to be a druggist, giving out medicine to sick people, and Mother will never want me to go so far away as China."

"I know," Grandfather admitted, "but God's call is higher than the parent's call."

"Well, I have doubts, too. Not about the call but about myself. I wonder if I have enough faith to be a missionary."

Hudson wondered if he

```
┌─────────┐   1. could trust God for health.
│  GUESS  │   2. could trust God for education.
└─────────┘   3. could trust God for money.
```

"You had best get these questions settled soon," Grandfather warned. "A missionary is made by

```
┌─────────┐   1. crossing the ocean."
│  GUESS  │   2. trusting God."
└─────────┘   3. getting a passport."
```

Grandfather thought trust in God was most important to missionaries. "But Hudson, you must do everything you can to ready yourself."

34

"I know," Hudson responded, "I'm getting ready for hardship. That's why I

	1. get more exercise."
GUESS	2. exchanged my featherbed for a hard mattress."
	3. eat less."

Not only did Hudson do those things, but he also gave up the evening church service and went to the poor parts of town to distribute tracts and talk to people.
Even more than that, he

	1. studied the Bible.
GUESS	2. prayed.
	3. studied the Chinese language.

Hudson did all that and then thought,

	1. *This is enough to prepare.*
GUESS	2. *I must do more.*
	3. *I should practice doctoring.*

When a chance came to go to the city of Hull and be an assistant to Dr. Hardey, Hudson said, "This is the preparation I need. I can learn to be a doctor and help people, too."
Hudson had a choice to live

	1. on Charlotte Street.
GUESS	2. with Dr. Hardey.
	3. at Drainside.

Hudson chose to live at Drainside with a poor old Christian lady, Mrs. Finch. As his landlady, she kept the small spare room clean and gave his breakfast. He supplied his other meals.

35

The Drain was a canal beside which poor cottages lined the road. There Hudson learned to

| GUESS |

1. endure hardness.
2. economize in order to help the poor.
3. live on oatmeal and rice.

He wrote Amelia, "The less I spend on myself, the more I can give to others. I cannot describe how I long to be a missionary and carry the Glad Tidings. Think, Amelia, every year twelve million souls in China die without God, without hope. I must leave as soon as possible. I feel as if *I cannot live* if something is not done for China."

All Hudson's life he had heard that

| GUESS |

1. God answers prayer.
2. God supplies all your needs.
3. all things work together for good.

But I must test myself, to see if I really do trust God. I must know that before I go to China, Hudson decided, and the opportunity for testing soon came.

Dr. Hardey admitted to being absentminded. "Hudson, you know how forgetful I am. When the time comes to pay your salary, you must remind me, or I'll forget."

Hudson wrote to Amelia, "Here is a chance to test my faith. I determined never to remind Dr. Hardey. I will only pray and trust God to remind the old doctor. If I cannot trust God with my money, I had best not even go to China."

Hudson was regularly rewarded with his paycheck until an especially busy season. Payday arrived, but Dr. Hardey said nothing. Hudson continued to pray. One Saturday night Hudson found himself with only a half-crown piece.* Still Dr. Hardey said nothing, and Hudson kept quiet.

He preached up and down Drainside the next day and was

---

*About a dollar at that time.

36

about to go home around ten o'clock when a poor Irishman stopped him. The man said,

GUESS

1. "I'm hungry."
2. "Come pray with my wife."
3. "I need money."

Hudson went at once with the fellow to his dying wife's side. "Why didn't you call a priest?" asked Hudson, knowing that would be the usual choice.

"The priest would not come without a payment of eighteen pence. My family is starving, and I have no work," the Irishman explained as he led Hudson down the dark street.

"Why did you allow things to become so serious? You could go to the relieving officer and get food," Hudson suggested.

"I did, kind Sir. He said to come tomorrow at eleven o'clock, but I fear my wife will not live through the night."

When they reached the wretched room, Hudson saw

GUESS

1. four starving children.
2. six diamond necklaces.
3. an exhausted mother and baby.

Hudson tried to comfort the starving family. He only had a half-crown piece. He had to give all or nothing. He choked. "You asked me to come and pray for your wife; let us pray."

He prayed, "Our Father Who art in heaven." During the prayer, Hudson's conscience reminded him, *Dare you mock God? Dare you kneel down and call Him "Father" with that half-crown in your pocket?*

When he rose from his knees, he slowly drew out the half-crown and gave it to the man. "It's all I have, but God is a Father who can be trusted to give you more."

At home his own words comforted him. *My Father in heaven can be trusted,* he told himself and fell asleep.

The next morning the landlady handed him a letter. Opening it, he found

GUESS	1. a blank sheet of paper.
	2. a pair of gloves.
	3. a handkerchief.

A pair of kid gloves fell out. When Hudson put his hand into one of them, he found a coin—a half sovereign.

"Four times as much as a half-crown!" Hudson marveled to his landlady.

The astonished woman cried, "If we are faithful to God in little things, He will be faithful to us in great things."

Hudson never did find out who sent the gloves. But he kept praying for payday. Finally, two Saturdays later, Dr. Hardey finished his reports and said, "By the way Taylor, is not your salary due again?"

Hudson admitted it was overdue.

"Oh, I'm so sorry. I sent all the money to the bank this afternoon. Otherwise, I would pay you at once."

Hudson knew he had nothing at home to eat. He knew his landlady expected the rent, but he said nothing and took his time finishing his work.

The doorbell rang as Hudson prepared to leave for home. The laughter of Dr. Hardey rang through the hallway. "Hudson, the strangest thing happened.

GUESS	1. A beggar gave me a penny.
	2. A rich patient paid his bill.
	3. A banker gave me a million pounds.

One of my richest patients has just come to pay his bill, Saturday night, ten o'clock, mind you. He had no check but paid with cash. He said he could not rest until his bill was paid." The doctor fumbled, hunting for a place to put the money.

"Taylor, you might as well take these notes. I have no change but can give you the rest next week."

Hudson went home to his little room. He wrote Amelia, "Thank the Lord, I can go to China. Now I know God will always answer prayer."

5

Shanghai

Though Hudson worked as an assistant to a doctor first in Hull and then in London, he kept writing to Amelia, "I feel as if I cannot live if something is not done for China."

He talked to the secretary of the Chinese Evangelization Society, telling him, "I want to go at once."

In 1853, the Tai-ping Rebellion seemed to have settled down, according to the news from China, and the society decided to send two men to Shanghai immediately.

Hudson was

GUESS	1. chosen as one of the men.
	2. told he must finish his preparation.
	3. told he was too young.

Hudson was accepted without finishing his medical training and assigned to the *Dumfries,* a sailing vessel, on September 19, 1853.

His mother came

1. to say good-bye.

GUESS

2. to beg him to stay.
3. hoping to change his mind.

As the ship moved out to sea, Hudson waved to his loving family. As they faded into the distance, he overheard a fellow passenger asking a sailor, "Why do they call you fellows 'limey'?"

"That started because the king of England ruled that sailors must suck limes to prevent scurvy."

Hudson laughed, "A new life begins."

During the five-and-one-half month trip, Hudson

GUESS

1. worried about the storms.
2. held gospel services for the sailors.
3. studied the Chinese language.

Hudson was pleased that many sailors accepted Christ during his services, but most of the time he prayed and studied.

On March 1, 1854, Hudson stepped ashore in China. He was met by

GUESS

1. a crowd of friends.
2. another missionary.
3. no one.

No one met Hudson in Shanghai. He was horrified to find the city in the grip of war. The "Red Turbans" ruled the city, and they fought continually.

Fortunately, he had written to the missionaries of the London Missionary Society, and they received him as a brother.

Dr. Lockhart asked him to remain as his guest; however, Hudson soon realized the Chinese Evangelization Society was sadly misinformed about conditions in China. His mission society sent neither money nor supplies.

They did, however, send another man, Dr. Parker, his wife, and three children. Hudson hurried to find a house in the native part of Shanghai. *We cannot impose on Dr. Lockhart further,* he thought. *The London Society should not be burdened with us.*

After a few weeks in native Shanghai, though, Dr. Parker's wife was frantic. She feared her children would be killed by the wicked natives stalking the streets with knives and guns. Dr. Parker said, "We must get out of this vile place! Everywhere we see killing."

When the house next door was burned, Hudson

GUESS

1. took the Parkers back to Dr. Lockhart.
2. sent them down the river.
3. sent them back to England.

A house in the foreign quarter belonging to the London Missionary Society had just become vacant, and Dr. Lockhart kindly welcomed them back to the mission compound.

Hudson and the Parker family gratefully moved at once, though they were short of money after paying the rent. There was no money to buy fuel to warm the house. Hudson had never been so cold. Though they were somewhat safe, they could look out their windows and see fighting in the streets below. He didn't know whether the children were shaking from fear or from cold.

"The committee in London doesn't understand our problem," Hudson told Dr. Parker.

"Well, how can they know coal costs fifty dollars a ton and food prices are impossible?" the doctor responded.

All the letters Hudson and Dr. Parker wrote

GUESS

1. got lost.
2. fell on deaf ears.
3. were answered.

Little money came from the Chinese Evangelization Society, and the good missionaries of the London Missionary Society often gave them food.

While waiting for peace, they learned the local Shanghai dialect. To be able to speak the language freely was necessary if they were to preach to the Chinese. Hudson and Dr. Parker studied diligently while they shivered from the lack of warm clothing and bedding. Friends helped when they could.

Hudson wrote Amelia, "You ask how I get over my troubles. This is the way . . . I take them to the Lord."

When the hot days of summer came, Hudson said, "We cannot preach on the streets of Shanghai because of the war, but we can take to the river in a houseboat. The country people living beside the river or in small villages also need the gospel."

"Let's go!" Dr. Parker, too, was ready. The Bible society sent New Testaments and Scripture portions in abundance.

Hudson said, "These people have never heard the way of salvation. How can they hear unless we go? They will perish in hell if no one tells them the good news."

"Let's go!" repeated Parker. So in spite of war, heat, or cold, he and Hudson made

GUESS	1. two journeys.
	2. six journeys.
	3. ten journeys.

They made ten journeys and learned the language of the country Chinese people. During the first three months, they

GUESS	1. gave away 1,800 New Testaments.
	2. gave away over 1,000 Scripture portions.
	3. gave away over 2,000 books and tracts.

They gave all of those to interested natives who could read.

Everywhere they went, crowds gathered. Their dress, their shoes, and their hair seemed strange to the Chinese. Dr. Parker said, "I don't see how you get to talk about anything but your hair."

"I know," Hudson groaned. "Everywhere the Chinese gather and ask about my red hair. They have never seen red hair before, I guess."

"It is a great hindrance to the preaching," Parker added.

"That is true, but God knew the color of my hair when He called me. What can I do about it?" Hudson was serious, but Dr. Parker laughed.

He said,

GUESS
1. "Who would think red hair could cause so much trouble?"
2. "You should dye it black."
3. "Shave it all off."

Hudson smiled. "You know it is not just my hair that hinders the preaching. They also ask about our clothes. We *could* change our clothes. What do you think?"

"Speak for yourself!" Dr. Parker roared. "I can't see myself in a Chinese gown! They probably don't make one large enough for me. No Chinese is over six feet."

Taylor looked serious. "I never thought I'd be glad for my small, thin figure. I'm the same size they are. God knew that, too. I'll pray about the clothes."

Sometimes Dr. Parker couldn't go on the journeys, and Hudson was lonely. He moved among unfriendly crowds and soon found his medical knowledge of the greatest value in gaining trust.

One night he could not sleep. He left the houseboat on the river and climbed to the top of a nearby hill. There he saw temples to Buddha and ancient pagodas. As he looked down, he said, "I can see the homes of millions who have never heard the name of Jesus. How can one man hope to reach so many?"

Then he looked again, for in the distance he saw clouds of

GUESS
1. fog.
2. smoke.
3. an approaching storm.

The cloud was smoke. Soon he saw a reddish glow in the sky. *Shanghai is in flames,* he thought, speeding back to his houseboat. *I must go there at once.*

Ash fell over the boat and covered the water with a gray scum. As he sailed toward Shanghai, he met fleeing rebels, who were caught and beheaded by the Turbans before his eyes. Everywhere he saw ruin. Hudson prayed and worried about the city and the London Mission.

Could that be Shanghai on fire?

When he finally reached the foreign section of Shanghai, he found

┌─────────┐   1. everything burned.
│ GUESS │   2. the people killed.
└─────────┘   3. that all was safe.

The Chinese Imperialists were too busy winning the war to bother the strangers. All were safe in the foreign compound.

Hudson wrote to Amelia, "Shanghai is now in peace, but it is like the peace of death."

6

Chinese Style

On one of their journeys, Hudson and Dr. Parker became acquainted with Mr. Jones and his group of American and British missionaries. The group was determined to build a hospital in Ningpo, and Dr. Parker was their choice as director.

When the London Missionary Society found it necessary to use their house for incoming missionaries, Dr. Parker and Hudson were notified they must move. At that point, Dr. Parker decided to accept the offer to become director of the Ningpo Hospital.

That left Hudson homeless. The Chinese Evangelistic Society contributed little in the way of support, and Hudson felt the London Missionary Society had helped him enough.

"Dr. Lockhart," Hudson said, "you have been very kind and helpful, but I feel God wants me to make a change. I've decided to

| GUESS |

1. wear Chinese clothes."
2. move to Shanghai."
3. eat Chinese food."

Hudson decided to do all those things.

"That's a mistake!" Dr. Lockhart replied. "You need to be identified as an Englishman. It is undignified to dress in Chinese clothes! How can you keep respect?"

"I feel this is what God desires of me. I have already bought the clothes."

"Very well." Dr. Lockhart sighed. "I've tried to help you, but if you won't listen, go your way, and may heaven help you!"

Hudson turned toward the native city and walked away. He felt

GUESS
1. sorrowful.
2. sad.
3. glad.

Hudson was sorry to disappoint a good friend but glad to follow Jesus. As he wandered the streets of Shanghai, a Chinese stranger touched him on the sleeve. "Are you seeking a house for rent?"

Hudson nodded.

"Would a small one do, and in the Chinese city?"

Seeing Hudson's interest, he went on, "Because near the South Gate there is such a house, only it is not quite finished building."

"How is this possible?" Hudson could not believe his ears.

The stranger answered, "The owner ran short of money and does not know how to complete the work."

Hudson followed the man

GUESS
1. as if in a dream.
2. suspicious it was a trick.
3. afraid he was being led to robbers.

Whatever he thought, they found a small, clean house with two rooms upstairs and two on the ground floor. A courtyard and guest room were across the way.

"Thank You, Lord Jesus," Hudson whispered. "Now I know my work in Shanghai is not finished." He spent most of his money for six months' rent.

Soon he moved in and proceeded to take the next big step. He

1. put on Chinese clothes.

48

GUESS

2. put on a space suit.

3. shaved his head.

Hudson put on Chinese clothes and went to a Chinese barber. The barber shaved the front of Hudson's head, darkened his remaining red hair to black, and braided it into a short queue. Then he fastened a long black braid to it.

Completing his outfit with satin shoes, he would pass in Shanghai as a "teacher," a man of the scholarly class.

As he left the barber shop,

GUESS

1. no one noticed him.

2. he looked like a clown.

3. he felt strange but comfortable.

Hudson certainly felt strange. He was not recognized as a foreigner until be began to preach or distribute books.

He went home and wrote letters telling of his changes. Besides writing to Amelia, he wrote to a Mr. Berger, who had sent a small money gift to further the work.

He also wrote to the Chinese Evangelization Society. He told

GUESS

1. of the changes.

2. why Dr. Parker had gone to Ningpo.

3. of future plans.

Hudson wrote all those things and thanked God for His guidance. Then he went to sleep on his Chinese floor mat.

Hudson's first convert was Kwei-hwa, who said, "Yes, I believe. I believe the true and living God, not idols."

Kwei-hwa studied, listened, and prayed. He followed Hudson like a shadow. Soon he brought his friends and relatives. A little group began meeting in the downstairs rooms, and Hudson taught them faithfully. Others now became interested.

In time Kwei-hwa became a Christian teacher himself, and Hudson felt free to leave the little group with him, while Hudson himself traveled inland up the Changjiang River.

Taylor hated to leave his faithful little flock, but, "How shall those farther on ever hear if we do not go inland?" he asked.

Taylor took a faithful Chinese missionary, and the two pushed their boat into the broad waters preparing to go up the river.

"I say, are you a missionary?"

Hudson looked up to see who was addressing him. In the next boat stood a man in European dress, smiling and waving his hands.

"I'm Hudson Taylor, Chinese Evangelization missionary!"

"And I'm William Burns, preacher from Scotland and Canada. Since we are headed up the Changjiang, let's keep our boats together for a ways. Bless my soul, I want to talk to a missionary in Chinese dress."

Like Paul and Timothy, Mr. Burns and Hudson soon became fast friends. Mr. Burns had a system for reaching a city:

GUESS	1. preach on the outskirts.
	2. visit temples, schools, and tea shops.
	3. invite those interested to the boat.

Those were the three steps Mr. Burns explained. "Many accept Christ on the houseboat. We say, 'Hao, ni hao'—'Good, you good!'—together."

Hudson listened and said, "Could we work together, do you think?"

"Let's try."

Mr. Burns noticed that the Chinese

GUESS	1. listened eagerly to Hudson.
	2. invited Hudson into their homes.
	3. asked Burns to wait outside.

As Mr. Burns waited outside while Hudson was invited in, he mused, "It's the Chinese clothes; I'll always be a foreigner in these clothes I'm wearing."

In December 1855, Mr. Burns also put on Chinese clothes, and

50

he and Hudson worked together up and down the river for seven happy months.

Hudson wrote to Amelia, "William Burns is better to me than a college course. He lives before me, right here in China, the reality of all I need to be and know. He is a spiritual father to me. He says, 'Joy is not in things; it is in us.' "

They went to Swatow where their reception was so great that they determined to start a hospital.

"Hudson," Mr. Burns instructed, "you go back to Shanghai and get the medical supplies we need. Bring all your medical equipment, for we will need everything."

So Hudson left Mr. Burns in Swatow and returned to Shanghai. When he got back to his little house, he found

GUESS

1. the city in flames.
2. his friends gone.
3. his medical supplies destroyed.

"What happened?" he cried.

Kwei-hwa replied, "We had a fire, and the room with the medical supplies burned. It was an accident."

As though that were not enough, he received word that Mr. Burns had been arrested and taken to Canton. Furthermore, they were both forbidden to return to Swatow. Hudson prayed for guidance. Sadly, he set out for Ningpo to continue his missionary work and visit Dr. Parker.

At Ningpo he heard more news:

GUESS

1. England and China were at war.
2. Swatow was a hotbed of hate for the English.
3. Men had landed on the moon.

Hudson was shocked, "England and China are at war! What a blessing Mr. Burns and I are not at Swatow where the Cantonese would surely kill us."

Hudson was reminded

| GUESS |

1. that all things work together for good.
2. that God answers prayer.
3. that he should always trust and obey.

He must have remembered all those things.

7

Maria

Besides acting as director of the new hospital, Dr. Parker treated many wealthy Chinese in Ningpo. "Nothing in the Bible says we cannot minister to the rich as well as the poor," defended Dr. Parker. "Actually, the fees paid by the rich are supporting the hospital, paying the nurses, and helping with the supplies. I find it a good arrangement."

"Yes, I see," Hudson said, "but what of the dispensary down on Bridge Street?"

"That is being neglected. Will you

GUESS

1. live there?
2. work there?
3. run away?

Hudson agreed to work there since patients were now coming.

"I can't leave town with this war going on, anyway. So this may be the place God wants me. I'll go now, and pray about it later." Hudson started to walk away.

"By the way, someone else is interested in working down there," Dr. Parker went on. "One of the teachers from our school is organizing night classes in child care, also hoping to reach women for Christ."

"I'm Maria Dyer."

"Who is he?" asked Hudson.

"He is a she—Maria Dyer. You will like her."

Hudson left the neat mission hospital compound and walked the two miles into the city to Bridge Street. It was easy to find the dispensary among the Chinese shops because of the large sign Dr. Parker had erected: "Free Dispensary for Sick Peoples." The line of sick people had indeed formed outside the door.

Hudson

| GUESS |

1. unlocked the door.
2. began seeing patients.
3. told them to go away.

Hudson was thankful for Dr. Hardey, who had taught him how to treat patients. He began at once. Usually the ills were minor. If a complicated case puzzled Hudson, he referred that person to Dr. Parker.

After the last patient walked out into the gloomy evening, a young woman opened the door. She wore a yellow dress with a long, full skirt. It had been years since Hudson had seen blonde curly hair and blue eyes. "I'm Maria Dyer." The young woman laughed.

"And I'm Hudson Taylor—"

"The new Chinese doctor with the funny eyes, or so your patients told me as they came out the door."

"They did? Why do they think I have funny eyes?" Hudson didn't exactly like being laughed at by this bubbling young woman.

"You don't know you have round eyes?" questioned Maria.

"That's nothing—so do you," Hudson replied indignantly. "All Europeans have round eyes."

"The Chinese don't know that. They see your Chinese clothes, your queue, and they think it strange your eyes are round instead of slanting. Don't feel bad. They call Westerners 'ocean ghosts' and Europeans 'big noses.' " Maria's laugh was a clear ripple that seemed to come from her heart. "May I ask why you wear Chinese dress?"

Hudson explained, "It is the Chinese people I want to reach. I want to put off all hindrance to our communication."

"I know what you mean," Maria responded. "Usually it is the language that hinders, but you seem to do so well. The Chinese didn't mention that in telling me all about you."

"My only trouble is with their expressions. They have one— 'Cat gone, old rat comes out.' It doesn't make sense, but they keep saying it," Hudson continued.

"You don't see the sense? You've never heard, 'When the cat's away, the mice will play'?"

" 'Cat gone'? Oh, I see, I see it all now. 'Old rat comes out.' " Hudson and Maria laughed together.

"Another thing they say is 'Seven hands, eight feet.' Now what could that possibly mean?" Hudson asked.

" 'Too many cooks spoil the broth,' " answered Maria. "Get it, Hudson?"

Hudson got it. He also knew he enjoyed this joyous young woman. "What are you doing?" he asked her.

"I'm preparing lunch. Dr. Parker told me you were here with no food. Since I was coming down here to clean out the storeroom anyway, I brought you something to eat," Maria answered.

"Splendid idea. I'm really hungry, and I'll help you with the storeroom. How many rooms does this place have, anyway?" Hudson questioned.

"Look around while I finish the lunch."

Hudson was impressed with the rather large building. Upstairs there were two rooms. The few items of furniture indicated a bedroom and sitting room. "Just what I need until the war is over," Hudson observed.

After they thanked the Lord for their food, Hudson and Maria ate their first meal together.

Hudson told a story. "In China long ago, a poet said of beautiful Hsi Chi that when she went for a walk fish dived deeper, geese swooped off their course, and deer ran into the forest before her beauty. Instead of saying, 'Beautiful as Hsi Chi,'' in Chinese one says, 'Diving fish, swooping geese'; but to you, Maria, I say, you are as beautiful as Hsi Chi.''

Maria changed the subject because

| GUESS | 1. she didn't know what to say. |
| | 2. she was embarrassed. |

56

3. she didn't want to hear more.

She was a little embarrassed.

"I thought of another Chinese saying" she said; "Fu Chien's army stopped the river's course when each soldier threw in his whip." Maria looked mischievous. "Can you guess that one?"

Hudson guessed,

GUESS

1. "Eenie, meenie, minie, mo."
2. "Little drops of water make a mighty ocean."
3. "Great oaks from little acorns grow."

Hudson couldn't think how a river's course could be changed by a soldier's whip.

"Not one whip, Hudson, thousands of whips—" Maria began.

"Oh, I see. Like millions of drops of water make a mighty ocean," Hudson finished.

"Right. And that's the way with this work on Bridge Street. I see the Chinese already like you, so you can reach them one by one. As your medicines help them, they'll come back for Bible study," she stated. "As my women come to learn about sanitation and child care, I can encourage them to also attend Bible study. One by one, as little drops of water, God will touch souls."

"You have a beautiful vision, Maria. I'll work with you as long as possible."

But Miss Aldersey, principal of the mission school, was not pleased. "You are seeing too much of that Taylor person, Maria. Remember you will be my main teacher once your sister marries."

"Miss Aldersey, Hudson is a fine Christian missionary," Maria exclaimed. "Why do you dislike him so?"

Miss Aldersey answered,

GUESS

1. "He wears Chinese clothes."
2. "His salary is paid with borrowed money."
3. "He isn't a suitable friend."

57

Hudson, too, was bothered because the Chinese Evangelistic Society borrowed money for his salary—when he got a salary. He had read in the Bible, "Owe no man anything."

"God is not poor," he told Maria. "God is not unwilling to supply our needs. I have tested Him myself and know I can trust Him."

Hudson worked on Bridge Street until his friends in Shanghai begged him to return. "The streets are safe, and two chapels need preachers," Kwei-hwa wrote. "Please help us!"

Back in Shanghai, Hudson

GUESS

1. preached in the city temple.
2. helped feed famine refugees.
3. ministered to the sick.

Besides doing all those things, Hudson thought about Maria. He told himself, *But I have nothing to offer her.* He talked to Kwei-hwa about her.

Kwei-hwa advised, "Never marry if you can help it. But I can see you are in love. We have a saying, 'Even with his eyes open, he can't see Mount Tai.'"

Hudson prayed and dreamed. Finally he wrote to Maria asking to marry her, even though he had resigned from the Chinese Evangelistic Society in June 1857.

In delight, Maria showed the letter to Miss Aldersey, hoping for her approval.

"Mr. Taylor! That nobody! Now that he has resigned, he has no one to pay his salary. How dare he suggest such a thing. Refuse him at once!"

Poor Maria

GUESS

1. cried.
2. argued with Miss Aldersey.
3. wrote a letter refusing the proposal.

Maria dared not disobey her principal. She remembered promising her dying father to obey the missionaries. In agony she wrote a letter dictated by Miss Aldersey. It was a definite and final no.

As soon as possible, Hudson returned to Ningpo but could only pray for an opportunity to see Maria. The opportunity came one July afternoon in the Jones' parlor. Several other people were in the room, but Hudson and Maria didn't notice.

"Maria, dear, may I write to your guardian in London for your hand?" Hudson expressed the speech he had memorized. Then he looked into Maria's eyes, saw her love, and kissed her. "Will you marry me?"

Maria looked around to see that Miss Aldersey was not near. "Only my guardian can overrule the principal, but I do love you, Hudson," she whispered.

Hudson looked at the group of people. He held Maria close and said, "Let us take it to the Lord in prayer."

best of earthly gifts." Like the Chinese, Maria called Hudson "prince of the house," and Hudson called Maria "the inside person."

Maria

GUESS	1. made a home on Bridge Street.
	2. worked in the mission.
	3. stopped teaching for Miss Aldersey.

Miss Aldersey turned her school over to a Presbyterian mission, and Maria continued to teach there part-time. She also worked at the dispensary.

Hudson

GUESS	1. remained faithful to the sick people.
	2. taught Bible classes.
	3. helped the new believers.

One of the new converts was Mr. Ni, formerly the president of an idolatrous society. He had heard the ringing of the bell on Bridge Street calling the people to Bible study. He entered the building to see what was happening.

Hudson was teaching about Moses lifting up the serpent in the wilderness. "For God sent not his Son into the world to condemn the world; but that the world through him might be saved."

At the close of the meeting, Mr. Ni rose and said,

GUESS	1. "I have tried to find the truth."
	2. "I have found no rest."
	3. "I am a believer in Jesus tonight."

We don't know what he said, but Mr. Ni became a student of the Bible and took Hudson with him to an idolatry meeting, where Mr. Ni

GUESS	1. preached the gospel.
	2. told the people he was a Christian.
	3. encouraged several to believe in Christ.

Ni became a great soul winner. One day he asked,

GUESS	1. "Is there a superman?"
	2. "How long has your country known of Christ?"
	3. "Did your ancestors worship Jesus?"

Hudson admitted his country had known of Christ for hundreds of years.

"What! Hundreds of years? My ancestors sought the truth and died without finding it. Why did you not come sooner?"

Mr. Ni was not the only convert. Ning-kuli, the basket maker; Wang, the grass cutter; and Wang-tsu, the house painter, and his mother all became soul winners among the Chinese.

As hatred for the English grew, the little building on Bridge Street was ransacked by lawless bands. Hudson knew who the leader was and sent him a letter.

"I understand you sold the things you stole for £40. Remember, your conscience looks in every time you hide a sin. All is forgiven; come hear the gospel and be saved."

The thief merely laughed and took the letter to the mission, where he put it in Dr. Parker's mailbox.

Dr. Parker sent it to England with a note telling everyone of Hudson's work and his forgiving spirit.

The letter was read by

GUESS	1. George Müller.
	2. Mr. Berger.
	3. Amelia.

Unknown to Hudson Taylor, his letter to the thief was read by

George Müller, pastor of Bethany Chapel and founder of orphans' homes. Mr. Berger, a manufacturer, also read the letter and determined to help Hudson in spite of the Opium War that was going on in China.

The summer after Hudson's marriage, the Treaty of Tientsin was signed, giving the English more control. Foreigners could now travel more freely and go openly to the interior of China—or so the treaty said.

Hudson wrote to England,

GUESS

1. "Send missionaries."
2. "Send doctors."
3. "Send the queen."

Hudson begged for missionaries and doctors for the Chinese people. He and Maria were busy and happy with their growing crowd on Bridge Street.

Their happiness was saddened, however, when Dr. Parker's wife sickened and died.

The dear doctor was doing such good work as director of the hospital. He was a blessing to all. But after Dr. Parker's wife died, he took his four children home to Scotland. The wards at the hospital were full of patients. Streams of people came for help. No other doctor was free to take the director's place. Everyone turned to Hudson Taylor.

"Will you be the director?" asked Mr. Jones, the leader of the Ningpo mission.

"You know I have no medical degree." Hudson was sorry he had not attended medical college. "Often I referred patients to Dr. Parker because I did not know the treatment."

"Will you be the director until we can find a qualified doctor? Please do it for me. Say yes, dear friend."

"If God wills, I'll do my best," Hudson promised. "The Golden Rule is to be lived, not learned."

When he told Maria, she objected. "But Hudson, how will the bills be paid? You know Dr. Parker treated the wealthy Chinese and charged fees. You can't do that without a doctor's diploma."

She continued, "How will the nurses' salaries be paid? What of supplies, not to mention your salary? Who will pay for it all? Do you know?"

"Yes," Hudson replied softly.

"Well, who?"

"God. Remember, Maria, I told you God would provide. You were surprised that I wrote to the Chinese Evangelization Society."

"Oh, yes, I remember you told them not to borrow any more money for your salary."

Hudson went on, "Have we lacked anything this past year?"

"No," Maria replied, "God always sent enough. Even the new believers were happy to share with us."

"Then why do you doubt God will provide for the hospital?"

Maria answered, "I see I must pray harder. It is harder to *do* right than to *know* right."

When Dr. Parker's assistants heard of the changes, some said,

GUESS	1. "There is money for only one month."
	2. "I'm going to quit right now."
	3. "I'll wait and see what happens."

Several assistants quit. A few nurses also said they couldn't work, not knowing if they would be paid. Even the patients wondered what would happen.

When the Bridge Street Christians heard that,

GUESS	1. they offered to help.
	2. they were afraid.
	3. they prayed.

Not only did they pray, they helped. Maria stopped teaching and acted as a nurse's aide. It was easy for her since she had helped with the dispensary on Bridge Street.

By the end of the month, Wang, the grass cutter, and Wang-tsu, the painter, were efficient workers on the wards. Maria's women transformed the place with their cheerfulness and faith. Others helped. The patients waited to see what would happen as they saw the supplies running low.

Finally the new cook appeared. "Master," he said, "the last bag of rice has been opened."

"Then the Lord's time to help is here," Hudson answered.

That day a letter arrived from England. "I have heard of you, Hudson Taylor. You are truly a man of God. My father left me a fortune, and the Lord has impressed me that you may know of a way to use the £50 I am enclosing. May I send you more? Your friend, W. T. Berger."

The Chinese said,

GUESS

1. "Can idols do that?"
2. "Can idols deliver us in our trouble?"
3. "Can idols answer prayer?"

They thought all that. After nine months, sixteen patients had been baptized, and more than thirty others had joined the Christian churches.

But

GUESS

1. Hudson Taylor's health failed.
2. Maria became ill.
3. no doctor came.

9

Surrender

After two-and-one-half years as director of the hospital at Ningpo, Hudson's health failed. Not only he, but also Maria, was too sick to care what happened to them.

Wang, the grass cutter, said, "They must be taken to England where they can get proper care, or they perish."

Wang-tsu, the painter, by now an excellent orderly and nurse, said, "I will take them."

Lae-djun, another believer, said, "Please excuse me. I also will go and help."

Hudson was in a daze as he and Maria went down the river to Shanghai and across the ocean to England.

Hudson was going

GUESS	1. home to his mother.
	2. to Amelia's new home.
	3. to #1 Beaumont Street, East London.

W. T. Berger heard of the emergency and arranged for an apartment on Beaumont Street. Wang-tsu and Lae-djun cared tenderly for the missionaries and nursed them back to health.

Maria recovered first and was proud to present Hudson with a fine son. By the time Hudson recovered enough to look around the apartment, Maria and Wang-tsu had made it into a home.

Slowly Hudson regained his strength.

"The first thing to do is to send a doctor to Ningpo to direct the hospital," Hudson said, knowing he could not go himself.

Maria answered,

GUESS

1. "But who will go?"
2. "We know no one."
3. "God will send someone."

She and Hudson prayed, "God send someone."

And it happened. James Meadows sailed for China in 1862.

Now Hudson turned to other work. His health permitted him to sit for several hours a day, and the Bible society asked him to revise the Chinese New Testament. He worked long hours on that dreary street in the poor part of London. Somehow he felt cut off from the world. He felt dull and weak. *Why must I suffer so?* he asked himself.

As soon as he could walk outside, he stumbled around the block, holding onto Lae-djun. The bustle of the city, the cries of the cabbies, and the noise of the children made him feel

GUESS

1. alone.
2. alive again.
3. weary of suffering.

Slowly he began to feel alive again and shocked Maria by attending classes at the medical school.

"You're twenty-nine years old and sick!" objected Maria.

"I was in such a hurry to go to China I did not prepare properly. You don't know how often I wept inside because I did not know how to operate or treat complicated diseases."

Maria said no more. She knew

1. Hudson had prayed.

GUESS

2. Hudson would obey God.

3. God would take care of him.

Together with Lae-djun, Hudson continued revising the Chinese New Testament. He placed helpful notes at the bottom of the pages. He obeyed God.

As soon as they were strong enough, Hudson and Maria visited Amelia on the west end of London.

"This is my husband, Bay Broomhall." Amelia beamed. "I'm so happy you two can talk together at last. We both enjoy your letters."

Maria and Hudson attended church with the young couple. Later they all ate lunch and played with Maria and Hudson's new baby.

Hudson tried to tell of his adventures in China but soon wearied. "Tell me about it another time, Hudson," Bay suggested. "I see our wives are talking so fast they may never finish the dishes."

It was true that Maria and Amelia talked. Mostly they talked about

GUESS

1. Hudson's red hair.

2. Hudson's Chinese dress.

3. Hudson's sickness.

They may have talked about all these things. Amelia told of Hudson's being teased about his red hair as a child. "I notice how short his hair is now," Amelia said.

"That is because it is just growing out. It looks strange to me since I have only seen him with a Chinese braid," Maria added.

They laughed together, and then Amelia grew serious. "What does the doctor say of Hudson's health?"

"He says Hudson will never be strong enough to return to China, but Hudson pays no attention to him," Maria explained.

"Sounds like my brother!"

"What sounds like me?" Hudson opened the door. "Aren't you finished in the kitchen yet? We must be going, Maria."

"Yes, you look tired," she agreed, gathering up the baby's things. She put on her warm cloak. The London fog chilled her to the bone.

Soon Hudson began going to the London churches and enjoying fellowship with Christians he met.

A pastor suggested to Hudson,

GUESS	1. "Write an article about the hospital." 2. "Take a vacation." 3. "Get some rest."

After the pastor read two of Hudson's articles, he said, "This is too important a work for our small paper. Why not enlarge this into a booklet telling of the needs of all of inland China, not just Ningpo?"

"Do you think people care?" asked Hudson.

"After reading your booklet, they'll care! You will see."

Hudson

GUESS	1. put a map of China on his wall. 2. wrote the booklet. 3. wept over the few missionaries there.

Hudson put up a map of China and studied it carefully. He researched the needs of every part of China. Then he wrote the booklet.

"It is not the seacoast that needs missionaries. It is the inland areas. I did not realize what a small area I had reached until I studied the map."

Hudson explained the needs to Wang-tsu and Lae-djun. Because they were both eager to learn, Hudson

GUESS	1. found Bible teachers for them. 2. prayed for them. 3. encouraged them to speak English.

70

Hudson prayed, and God provided Chinese Bible teachers for the men, who studied faithfully.

Daily as he faced the map of China, Hudson prayed for workers for all of China. "Many workers are needed," he told Maria.

Another son was born, and Maria laughingly told Hudson, "See, God is sending workers! Does not the Bible say, 'Seek ye first the kingdom of God, and his righteousness; and all these things shall be added unto you'?"

Hudson smiled at his wife and touched her hair. "We have been blessed with two fine red-headed sons, and I do pray they may in time be workers for China. However, the present need is for

| GUESS |

1. twenty-four missionaries."

2. an organization to send them."

3. money to meet the needs."

Hudson puzzled over the shortage of missionaries. "Because of a lack of money, there is no missionary society to send workers to China," he lamented. "At least not to inland China."

"No one seems to care," Maria added.

Hudson was still puzzling over the problem when he received an invitation

| GUESS |

1. to the beach.

2. to the mountains.

3. to Mars.

The invitation was for a week's stay at Brighton. "The ocean breeze will do wonders for your health," Mr. Pearce, one of Hudson's new-found friends, urged.

So Hudson left the heavy heat of London for the surf and the sand of Brighton Beach. He was never the same again.

As he walked in the sand, the soft breeze blowing against his face felt like a caress from heaven. Hudson felt like talking to the Lord.

"I see the needs of the Chinese, Lord," he said, "and I am too small to meet those needs."

Hudson stopped walking, looked at the endless ocean, and thought of the power of God. "You have shown me Your power in supporting me on the mission field, but twenty-four missionaries are now needed. Do You have the power to support twenty-four? Is there anyone who can do that? Someone is needed who

GUESS	1. sees the need."
	2. trusts Jesus."
	3. will start a new missionary society."

Someone was needed who saw the need, trusted Jesus, and would start a new missionary society for inland China.

The conviction came to him as a full-blown rose, complete and perfect.

"You are the man!"

Hudson looked into the vast sky and said aloud, "Lord Jesus, if You want me for this service, I surrender."

Hudson's eyes shone with a quiet light.

He told Maria later, "There I surrendered myself to God for His service. I asked for twenty-four missionaries to take to China."

10

New Beginnings

"I want to tell Mr. and Mrs. Berger of God's call to me," Hudson told Maria upon his return to London.

"Shall we order a carriage to take us to Saint Hill?" Maria asked, knowing that a horse and carriage were only hired for important occasions.

"Yes, yes! Wang-tsu can care for the boys. We'll make it a day of celebration," Hudson answered.

Mr. and Mrs. Berger were delighted to see the young couple and concealed their surprise at this sudden visit. Their estate covered an entire hill, which was surrounded by the city. Mr. Berger's starch factory prospered, and he had no need for the inheritance left him by his father.

"What brings you out this chipper morning?" he asked.

As he and Hudson talked, they discussed

GUESS	
	1. the mission society.
	2. how to make the society known.
	3. how to attract missionaries.

They agreed the society was to reach only the inland parts of China. All donations were to be the result of God's speaking to individuals, not of fund-raising speeches or pledges.

"I'll tell of the society and interview the missionaries who apply. I'll take them to China and help them get settled," Hudson stated.

"And I'll keep the home fires burning, receive the donations, and send the money. We will only plan as much as God gives money for," Mr. Berger declared.

"We'll call it the China Inland Mission—CIM," they agreed. Both men knew their duties. God had called them both.

"Someone you must meet is George Müller," Mr. Berger said. "You could speak to his orphans. Some of them may be called as missionaries, you know." Mr. Berger winked at his wife. "We will write him a letter."

"You know who will write the letter." Mrs. Berger laughed. "If we wait for Mr. Berger, it will be never." Mrs. Berger and Maria gladly entered into the plans. They were as earnest in prayer and as eager to help as the men.

"You must move to a larger place where you can accommodate small groups of friends who want to hear of the plans," Mrs. Berger said.

"Also, you need a room in which to interview missionary candidates." Mr. Berger was enthusiastic. He had been praying about this for months.

The Taylors moved to spacious no. 30 Coburn Street.

While Wang-tsu cared for the children and the household, Maria became Hudson's hands.

She

GUESS

1. wrote letters.
2. prayed.
3. offered suggestions.

Maria helped in many ways.

Soon people called her "the Mother of the Mission."

When Hudson's little booklet was printed, Mrs. Berger sent it to all her friends. Within three weeks it had to be reprinted. Many people wanted copies for all the members of their churches.

Soon groups called on the Taylors at their home to inquire how they could help. Maria had lists of supplies needed for dispensaries, schools, and families.

Others wrote letters. Lord Radstock wrote, "I have been stirred by your pamphlet. Dear Brother, enlarge your desires! Ask for a hundred labourers, and the Lord will give them to you."

How shocked Hudson would have been had he known that in later years

| GUESS |

1. he *would* ask for one hundred workers.
2. God would send one hundred workers.
3. God would send more.

In later years Hudson would ask for one hundred workers in one year, and they all would go to China. But in 1866, Hudson asked only for twenty-four missionaries.

A man named Rudland read the pamphlet, prayed, and offered himself as a missionary. At his interview, Hudson Taylor asked, "When did you become a Christian?"

Mr. Rudland looked into Hudson's eyes and said, "I'm a blacksmith in Cambridgeshire village. My mother prayed for me, taught me, and took me to church, so I knew how to be saved. I just wasn't willing. Then one Saturday night I was in the farmhouse kitchen and happened to look at the calendar on the wall. There in big letters were these words: 'Now is the time, now is the day of salvation.' I knelt and asked Jesus to save a poor sinner like me."

"When did you feel called to China?" Hudson inquired.

"After I read your pamphlet, I prayed and prayed. I just couldn't get away from the idea that I should go," Mr. Rudland answered.

"Did anyone try to talk you into the idea?" Hudson went on.

"No, as a matter of fact, my employer showed me a Chinese book, saying, 'This is the way they talk over there. Do you think you could ever learn this?' "

Hudson questioned again, "What did you say?"

"I said if others learned it, why not I?"

Hudson looked at the earnest blacksmith. He trusted God to help him choose the missionaries. Both Hudson and Mr. Berger felt Rudland was a good candidate.

From Ireland Charles McCarthy and Edward Fishe came. Dr. Barnardo, also from Ireland, moved to London with Charles and Edward but felt God wanted him to open a training school for homeless children.

The eighteen missionaries chosen were

| GUESS |

1. from England.
2. from Ireland.
3. from orphanages.

Maria smiled. "Why are we taking eighteen instead of twenty-four? I thought you prayed for twenty-four."

"Eighteen missionaries, including Wang-tsu and Lae-djun, plus you and I make twenty. Our three boys and the son of one missionary couple make twenty-four. Right?" Hudson answered. "Unless you wish to stay here?" he teased.

"Nothing could keep me here; but I do hope our child is born before we leave. How do you know it will be a boy?" Maria could tease, too.

Later Hudson was called to a meeting at Totheridge. Colonel Puget, brother of Lady Radstock, had been persuaded by his sister to lead the meeting. The people at the meeting were friends of Lady Radstock. The meeting

| GUESS |

1. went well.
2. was discouraging.
3. was very long.

Everything went well. Hudson spoke to an interested audience, but when Colonel Puget wanted to take an offering, Hudson refused to allow it.

The colonel said, "You have made a great mistake. The people were interested and would have given a good sum."

Some of the people said, " 'Tis a foolhardy business."

"Not so foolhardy, as superhuman," others said. "You will be forgotten. Before long you may find yourselves without even the necessities of life."

Hudson answered, "I am taking my children with me. I do not find it difficult to remember they need breakfast, dinner, and supper. Why should our heavenly Father forget?"

The next morning as Taylor prepared to leave, the colonel said, "As I lay awake in the night, I thought of the stream of souls in China going to hell. I cried, 'Lord, what wilt Thou have me to do?' "

He

GUESS	1. handed Taylor a check for £500.
	2. gave him a five-pound note.
	3. offered to go to China.

The colonel said, "If there had been a collection, I would have given five pounds and forgotten about it. As a result of God's leading, there is a check for £500."

That was enough to secure accommodations on the *Lammermuir,* a ship leaving England on May 26, 1866.

When the ship sailed,

GUESS	1. all of Hudson's group was aboard.
	2. Hudson was happy.
	3. Hudson thanked God.

God had answered his prayers.

11

Dark Days

As the journey began, the missionaries in Hudson's party held prayer meetings. Carefully the sailors watched to see if what they said matched what they did. Finally the sailors asked for meetings.

Hudson's group

GUESS

1. refused.
2. gladly preached.
3. pretended not to hear.

Those meetings resulted in a large majority of the crew becoming Christians. Everyone rejoiced.

But soon the storms came. All the way up the China Sea they were pressed by storms and typhoons. Hudson wrote to Amelia, "After twelve days, the ship is rolling fearfully; the yards dangling and tearing our only sail. The roar of the water, the clanging of chains, the beating of masts and the smack of the torn sails make it impossible to hear."

For three more days, the storm

1. washed water aboard.

| GUESS |

2. put the fires out.
3. spoiled the drinking water.

The women as well as the men worked at the pumps, trying desperately to pump out the water as fast as it washed in.

Even so, the little *Lammermuir* limped into Shanghai in September. The sailors gave a parting gift of

| GUESS |

1. good will.
2. thank yous.
3. thirty pounds.

The sailors gave thirty pounds of their own money to the missionaries. "We will pray for you," they said. The sailors knew the pitfalls of a strange land better than the missionaries did.

The missionaries had

| GUESS |

1. literature and Bibles.
2. household goods and medical supplies.
3. printing and lithographic presses.

They had all that besides twenty-four people and their personal possessions. The Presbyterian Mission of Shanghai had an unused warehouse that they offered to Mr. Taylor.

Here the missionaries

| GUESS |

1. stored their things.
2. camped out.
3. changed clothes.

While still in London, all the new missionaries had promised to wear Chinese clothing once they were in China. Now, however,

1. some objected.

80

GUESS

2. some changed but grumbled.

3. some liked the new clothes.

Hudson was surprised at the grumbling. He was thankful everyone was safe.

The youngest missionary, a slip of a young lady, did the most to cheer the group. She loved the Chinese dress and pointed out the advantages:

GUESS

1. no tight belts.

2. no tight corsets.

3. no high-buttoned shoes.

"I feel so free and comfortable. No wonder the Chinese women prefer slacks and kimonos. I find them delightful."

"Oh, Miss Faulding, you look lovely, but I feel so very, very strange," moaned Mrs. McCarthy. "I feel as though I'm in my night clothes."

Four weeks later the whole party trooped onto houseboats. "We'll go up the river to Hangchow," Hudson decided. "That will be a hub from which we can circle out into the interior."

By now autumn had arrived. Several persons became ill. The nights on the water were bitterly cold, and the boat owners were anxious to be rid of the missionaries so they could go home for the winter.

"Maria," Hudson said, "I must find a comfortable place for this crowd. I see they don't all have the pioneer spirit of my little wife."

"Don't worry, Hudson," Maria reminded him. "God has directed us thus far. He won't fail us now."

Hudson parked the boats in a quiet place outside Hangchow and went alone to the city. There he found

GUESS

1. a furnished home.

2. room for all.

3. a dirty shack.

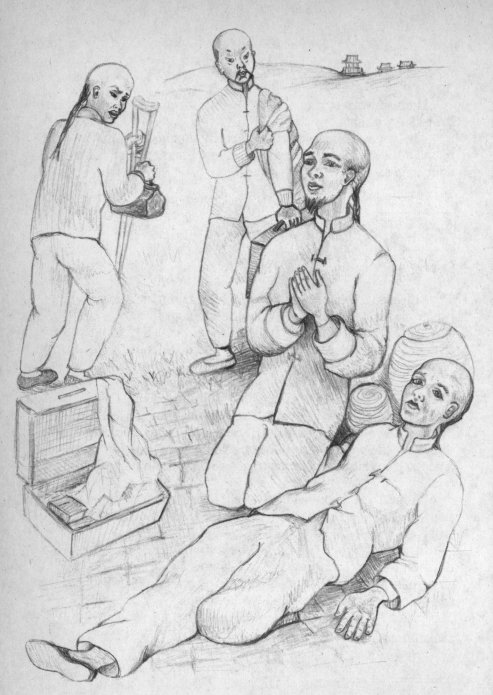

Robbers!

One of the Hangchow missionaries was absent for a week and left word that Hudson's party should make themselves at home. That night the weary travelers rested in comfort and warmth.

During the next week, Taylor secured a place of their own. A large old rambling house with many apartments was available and perfect for their purposes.

As soon as they had settled, Miss Faulding gathered a group of women into her apartment and in her broken Chinese taught them as best she could. They called her Miss Happiness.

The missionaries in Hangchow

GUESS

1. opened a hospital.
2. started a church.
3. helped 200 Chinese.

More than two hundred people attended the church and dispensary.

Hudson sat up at night, studied the maps, and made plans. He and Mr. Meadows had found opportunities for work in Siaoshan, and Mr. Meadows was anxious to get started.

Hudson and Mr. Duncan also followed the Yenchow River to Lan-chi, where Mr. Duncan proposed to stay. In a room with a shutter for a window, a mud floor with only a chair, bamboo trestles, a traveling rug, pillow, and mosquito net, he started his service for God. "How can I consider comfort when souls are lost and dying?" he told Hudson.

On one occasion Hudson accompanied one of his missionaries, who had only one leg. The man walked with a crutch. When they came to Wenchow, where rioters robbed them of everything, he was helpless without his crutch.

"Why don't you run away?" yelled the leader of the gang.

"Run away?" The missionary smiled. "How can a man run with only one leg, I should like to know?"

Hudson prayed, and suddenly the rioters left without taking their possessions. In time, that same missionary was working happily in Wenchow.

Wang-tsu went to Ningpo and carried on the work on Bridge Street. In fact, Ningpo served the China Inland Mission as headquarters from time to time.

During the summer of 1870, the Taylors sailed up the Grand Canal to Chin-Kiang, where Hudson tried to find a place to live.

The heat came, rain fell, and the Taylors took shelter in an inn. Maria was disturbed. "Hudson, something must be done for the baby. Let me take him to Shanghai for treatment."

"Very well," Hudson agreed, "and you can bring back Mr. Duncan's fiancée, who will arrive in Shanghai soon. Don't worry about the boys," he added. "Miss Blatchley can look after Howard and Sonny while you are gone."

Maria hurried on her way.

Confidently, Hudson sent word to Mr. and Mrs. Rudland to bring the printing presses to Chin-Kiang.

But no sooner had Maria taken the baby to the doctor and picked up Duncan's fiancée than she heard that Hudson himself was sick. She

GUESS

1. brought the baby back.
2. rowed the boat herself.
3. went on a vacation.

Taking the baby on the boat with the young woman, Maria rowed the boat herself when the boatman became tired. Only her determination kept the boat going the last few miles. Her strength was spent.

While Maria nursed Hudson, enemies were at work. They

GUESS

1. displayed signs asking people to set fire to the mission.
2. said two foreigners had stolen twenty-four children.
3. cried, "Foreign devils! Foreign devils!"

The opposition did all those things and gathered a crowd, which followed Mr. and Mrs. Rudland as they delivered the printing presses and household goods.

When Hudson opened the door for the Rudlands, the crowd surged forward and began breaking and stealing things. They

84

hustled Hudson about even though he was sick. Hudson called upstairs to Maria and the boys, "Flee! Flee!"

The boys exclaimed, "Come! This way. Out the window onto the roof."

Maria carried the baby, and Miss Blatchley followed the two boys as they stepped out the window.

"Come to this end!" Howard called. "We always jump from here. It's lower."

"What do you mean?" Maria stopped suddenly.

"Never mind," Miss Blatchley said, "just jump!"

Maria jumped. Her leg was hurt, and Miss Blatchley injured her back, but they all managed to sneak into the open door of the neighboring house.

Hudson, in the meantime, went to the authorities crying, "Save life! Save life!" The Mandarin (ruler) responded slowly. When the Taylors returned,

GUESS	1. everything was wrecked.
	2. some things were burned.
	3. the presses were scattered.

Their precious presses were scattered. The next day they were escorted out of town.

The neighbor who sheltered Maria sent an account of the riot to the Shanghai paper and demanded that the British authorities intervene.

Since the two boys were ill, the Taylors decided to send them to England with Miss Blatchley, who needed treatment for her back.

Maria also was sick but would not leave the work. In her weakened condition she contracted cholera. The day she heard the boys were safe in London, Maria and the baby died.

12

New Stations

Hudson felt empty at the loss of Maria and the absence of his boys. He

GUESS

1. worked harder.
2. was too busy to think.
3. could do nothing but cry.

Hudson flung himself into the labor of starting new mission stations. One day he got a letter from Mr. Berger. "It seems that someone wrote an account of the riots at Chin-Kiang, and they appealed to the British government for protection. You couldn't believe the way it has stirred up parliament. People are saying, 'Why don't they stay at home where it is safe? They can't expect British gunboats to make the Chinese change their religion.'"

The newspaper reports said

GUESS

1. the missionaries were causing war.
2. the missionaries wanted soldiers in China.
3. the missionaries converted Chinese at bayonet point.

All newspaper reports were false, but Hudson said, "You can get even by revenge, but you become superior when you pass it over."

Mr. Berger sadly reported the results.

GUESS	1. Many people believed the newspapers.
	2. Many people stopped giving money for the China Inland Mission.
	3. Many stopped praying.

But when Mr. Berger sent an account of money received at the end of the year, it was the same as the year before, even though many people refused to give.

The difference was given by

GUESS	1. George Müller.
	2. Bethany Chapel in Bristol.
	3. Jenny Faulding.

George Müller increased his personal gifts, and his chapel in Bristol also gave large sums.

In time the lies

GUESS	1. died.
	2. blew over.
	3. were smothered.

Nothing stopped the lies as well as the good news of God's blessing in China. After six years, the China Inland Mission

GUESS	1. had thirty stations in China.
	2. had ten stations in China.
	3. had twenty stations in China.

Thirty stations received God's blessing. Thirty foreign missionaries labored in peace, and fifty native Chinese worked for and preached the gospel of Jesus Christ.

In 1872 Hudson Taylor married Jenny "Happiness" Faulding and spent eighteen months in England. They were happy to see the boys once again. The boys called their new mother "Happie."

In London, Hudson was referred to as "our illustrious guest." Mr. Taylor replied, "Dear friends, I am the little servant of an illustrious Master." He asked everyone to pray for eighteen new missionaries for China.

They came back to China with

GUESS

1. eighteen new missionaries.
2. twenty-four new missionaries.
3. one hundred new missionaries.

In 1873, eighteen new missionaries returned with the Taylors. The world marveled at the success of this small, sickly man who had undertaken such an enormous task.

Hudson answered, "I don't look upon it that way. I sometimes think that God must have been looking for someone small enough and weak enough for Him to use, so that the glory might be His. He found me."

This time it was easier for the Taylors to place the eighteen new missionaries. When they visited the thirty stations they found

GUESS

1. illness.
2. new converts.
3. tired workers.

The tired workers welcomed Hudson, who inspired them to reach the unsaved. He prayed with them and treated their illnesses.

Going from station to station, he met all the workers, introduced the newcomers, and encouraged everyone. At one station, eighty-nine letters awaited him.

Jenny helped. The new women missionaries, especially, leaned on her for inspiration. They spent nine months in the Yangtse Valley and turned to the province of Che-Kiang.

One by one

GUESS	1. the missionaries were settled.
	2. new stations started.
	3. stars fell.

In time, many new stations were started, and all eighteen missionaries were at work. Then everything started to go wrong.

Miss Blatchley's health failed. That meant that there was no one to care for the boys in England. Mr. Berger retired. That meant the business affairs of the China Inland Mission had no leader. Funds were low. That meant that supplies would soon be exhausted.

"What shall we do?" Jenny asked.

"What a comfort it is to know that though supplies may be exhausted, our Supplier can never be exhausted," Hudson answered.

GUESS	1. "God wants us in England."
	2. "We'll follow the Yangtse River."
	3. "We'll find a ship."

Aboard ship, Hudson attempted to climb a ladder between decks. He slipped on one of the steps, fell, sprained his ankle, and injured his spine. A concussion of the spine and paralysis followed.

Jenny Taylor arrived in England with Hudson, a hopeless invalid.

13

Fruit of Suffering

In August 1874 Hudson found himself at 6 Pyrland Road, London. He was strapped to a board.

"Don't move," Jenny reminded him. "The doctor says, 'Don't move.' "

"But the pain is so, so—it takes my breath when it stabs me that way. I feel I must move!" Hudson groaned.

Hudson's boys, Howard and Sonny, were happy to be with their father and mother in a new home.

"Father," Howard, a tall lad of twelve, said. "I'll be the doorman and will usher the friends upstairs to your room."

"First put up the map of China," Hudson said.

"Where?" Howard questioned.

"Between the posts of the bed. There at the side. I want to see it so I can pray."

Howard first asked Jenny to sew a large hem across the top of the map. "See, the face is paper, but a cotton gauze has been glued on the back so it won't tear."

That done, he and Sonny threaded a small rope through the hem. Carefully they stretched the rope from bedpost to bedpost and tied each end with a knot.

"Sonny, your knot is *larger* than the bedpost." Hudson laughed.

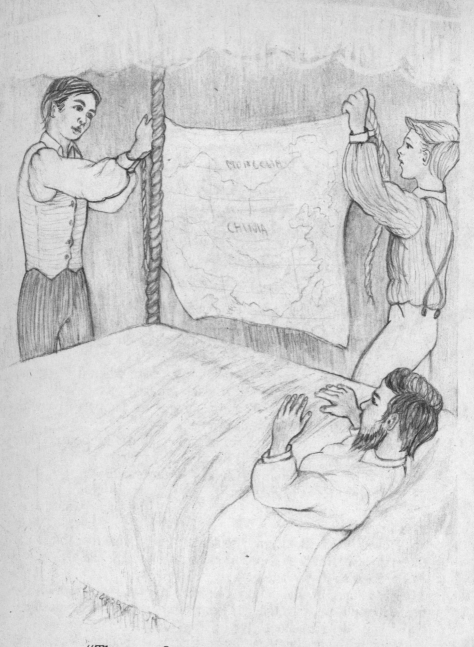

"There . . . I want to see it so I can pray."

"I tied it a third time because the other two knots were loose. It will hold now." Ten-year-old Sonny nodded in satisfaction, his red curls bobbing.

Watching his boys work with the rope reminded Hudson of something. *What is it?* he asked himself. *I feel like I've seen this before, but I've never been confined to a bed before.* Hudson puzzled for some time.

His first visitor of the morning was the Reverend W. G. Lewis. Together they

GUESS	1. rejoiced in the Lord.
	2. talked over old times.
	3. prayed together.

Pastor Lewis read Scripture and prayed. As he departed, he said, "Now, Hudson, is there anything I can do for you?"

"Oh, no," Hudson replied, "Jenny and the children care for me. Thank you!"

"Well, let me know if I can help. I mean that, Hudson."

Howard ushered Pastor Lewis downstairs and to the door just as Mr. Pearce rang the bell.

"I'm Howard Taylor; won't you come in?" invited the red-haired boy.

"I'd like to see your father," Mr. Pearce requested.

All day long a stream of visitors came and went: old Mr. and Mrs. Berger, who could hardly climb the stairs; a young man, F. W. Baller, whose name Howard forgot; Lord and Lady Radstock in their fine clothes; Miss Soltan; and, of course, Amelia with her five children.

"Children, you stay downstairs and play with Sonny. I won't be gone long," Amelia admonished.

Great was the rejoicing that day as prayers and good wishes were spoken. Often they told one another, "God's will be done!" Every person said,

| GUESS | 1. "Is there anything I can do?" |
| | 2. "Let me know how I can help." |

3. "I want to do something."

Hudson heard all those words many times.

Miss Soltan brought a bird in a cage. "I thought this little canary could sing to you," she said. "He is a cheerful songbird. I know—I've had him for over a year."

When everyone was gone, Howard took the supper dishes away, and Hudson was alone. He looked at the little bird tucking his head under his wing, ready for the night.

Suddenly, Hudson remembered, *Grandmother's birds. Never did I think I'd be like Grandmother,*

GUESS	1. *a helpless invalid.* 2. *utterly useless in this world.* 3. *unable to work.*

[Hudson felt useless.] *I feel like I'm floating along like a branch that spins in an eddy. The current takes it first this way, then that. Round and round in a useless circle. But what am I thinking! Grandmother wasn't helpless. She put up the birdhouses. I remember she did.*

But how? A picture came before Hudson's eyes as if in a dream. The word she sent out to the children; the materials she had ready; the organization she planned; the activity she supervised; and the thanks she waved with her one good hand.

"I have two good hands. Why am I whining? Forgive me, Lord. I see Your plan now."

Far into the night, Hudson prayed and planned. Never again did he complain about his suffering. "I see what Grandfather meant when he said, 'Out of suffering come God's greatest warriors,' " Hudson mused.

In the days that followed, he sent for his friends one by one. "You can do something for me and for God," he said. "Amelia, will you and Bay move to Pyrland Road and help with the mission?"

"Mr. and Mrs. Berger, you have said, 'Saint Hill is a burden.' Could you sell it and move to Pyrland Road where you can advise the new business manager of the China Inland Mission?"

To F. W. Baller, Hudson declared, "You just received your accounting degree. Will you manage the business office of the China

Inland Mission? You can count on Mr. Berger's experience."

"Miss Soltan, can you write letters and be the office helper Mr. Baller needs?"

"Mr. Broomhall, will you edit a magazine for the China Inland Mission?"

So it went; even Howard and Sonny had their tasks. But nothing was organized without prayer. Amelia and Bay surprised themselves by speaking to groups about the work of the China Inland Mission. They also worked hard on the magazine.

Hudson began to write again. Volunteers came each day to write for him. Afterward, Hudson said, "One of the happiest periods of my life was that period of forced inactivity, when I could do nothing but rejoice in the Lord and 'wait patiently.' Never were my letters before or since written so regularly and answered so promptly."

In January 1875, Jenny and Hudson together received £4000 from an unexpected source.

After prayer, Hudson inserted an article in a Christian paper: "Appeal for Prayer: on behalf of more than a hundred and fifty million Chinese."

The article told of the unevangelized areas and the aims of CIM and then stated: "Four thousand pounds have been received for the spreading of the Gospel. The urgent need is for missionaries, those willing to face any hardship for God."

Hudson asked the readers to pray for

GUESS	1. eighteen missionaries.
	2. twenty-four missionaries.
	3. one hundred missionaries.

Again Hudson asked for eighteen missionaries, and one by one they came to his upstairs room. Howard was delighted to escort them, show them the map, and hear the appeal of missions.

After the eighteen missionaries were accepted and the business department of the China Inland Mission was organized and the funds were collected, God raised up Hudson Taylor from his bed. His back was strong again.

God had kept Hudson in bed

GUESS

1. to mend his spine.
2. to glorify God.
3. to increase his faith.

Soon Hudson was speaking to Christian groups again. After one such meeting, a Russian nobleman stepped up to him. "Allow me to give you a trifle toward your work in China," the Russian said.

When Taylor saw the sum, he replied, "Did you not mean to give me five pounds? Please let me return this note; it is for fifty."

"I cannot take it back," replied the count, who was surprised. "Five pounds was what I meant to give, but God must have intended you to have fifty. I cannot take it back!"

When Hudson returned to Pyrland Road, he found the household in prayer. Money to be sent to China was short by more than £49. Taylor laid the £50 note on the table.

"God sent it," he said.

Again it seemed that Britain and China were going to war. Negotiations dragged on for months. It seemed impossible that violence could be stopped.

People told Hudson, "Don't go to China now. You will all have to return. It is out of the question!"

Hudson decided

GUESS

1. to wait.
2. to go.
3. to forget it.

Hudson decided to go. As the eighteen missionaries and the Taylors boarded ship, they heard that

GUESS

1. the viceroy had died.
2. the British minister had fainted.
3. the convention was signed.

96

The Chefoo Convention was signed, giving liberty of access to every part of China.

"Just as our brethren were ready—not too soon and not too late—the door opened." Hudson rejoiced.

14

Open Doors

This time placing the eighteen new missionaries was different. Every mission station begged for help. With the new government decrees, it was lawful to start outposts anywhere in China —not without struggle, however.

One of the new missionaries, George Nichol, was once with Hudson when word came of serious rioting in two older stations. When Hudson heard the news, he

| GUESS |

1. whistled a song.
2. fell on his knees.
3. cried.

George was astonished to hear Taylor whistling, "Jesus, I am resting, resting, in the joy of what Thou art; I am finding out the greatness of Thy loving heart." It was Hudson's favorite song.

George exclaimed, "How can you whistle when our friends are in so much danger?"

"Would you have me anxious and troubled?" Taylor replied. "That would not help them and would certainly hinder me. I have just to roll the burden on the Lord."

"I don't understand," George said.

"It is God's work, not mine. I've learned at last to rejoice in the Lord under all circumstances. I'm too weak to do this work; God does it through me."

When Wang-tsu, still faithfully working in Ningpo, said, "I think it wonderful that you accomplished so much while you were in England," Hudson replied, "Me? I could do nothing. I was helpless, strapped to a board. I was only able to turn over as Jenny or Howard pulled a rope. It was God who accomplished so much—not me!"

During the next two years, the pioneers of CIM traveled 30,000 miles throughout the inland provinces of China. Dozens of young missionaries had come to China alone. Now they wished

GUESS

1. to bring their sweethearts.
2. to marry.
3. to have homes in China.

All that was true. Many other single young women also desired to do mission work.

Hudson said to Jenny, "You came alone, and you are beloved of the Chinese. Your work has proven valuable. I don't see any objection to women missionaries."

"Neither do I, but you know there will be an outcry if women are allowed to go into the far interior. England will object loudly," Jenny warned.

"Let her object!" Hudson decided. When he encouraged women to come to China,

GUESS

1. a few came.
2. many came.
3. none came.

Many answered God's call to China. It was well, for a famine came to China in 1877. Six million people of North China faced starvation.

Hudson decided

GUESS	1. to go to England.
	2. to beg for help.
	3. to write a book.

The Taylors went to England to ask for aid for the starving Chinese. Hudson spoke to churches, wrote articles for the China Inland Mission magazine, and begged for helpers.

He told of

GUESS	1. children dying.
	2. parents dying, leaving orphans.
	3. girls sold into slavery.

Hudson wrote about all those conditions. People responded and gave money to rescue children, start orphanages, and feed the stricken.

Many wanted Hudson to carry out the projects. "I cannot; I'm sick in bed," Hudson answered. "But I'll pray for someone to go!"

Night after night he and Jenny prayed for someone to carry out the work. *Who will go?* they wondered.

Finally Hudson looked into Jenny's eyes. "You could go," he said. "You could set up the orphanages and organize the women who have volunteered to help. You could be God's hands to feed the starving!"

Jenny's face appeared like the face of the suffering world. "And what of you?" she asked softly.

"I'll be all right. Howard and Sonny can look after me," Hudson exclaimed.

"What of our two little children?" questioned Jenny.

"Amelia can care for them," Hudson responded.

"Really, Hudson, you know she has ten children of her own!"

"We can ask her," Hudson stated.

When Amelia was asked, she said,

GUESS	1. "I'll do it."
	2. "Are you crazy?"

3. "No, not in a hundred years!"

Amelia answered, "If Jenny is called to go to China, I am called to care for her children." She added the missionary's children to her own.

People wondered if Jenny Taylor was really called to feed the starving Chinese. "If she is called, God will show us," old Mr. Berger lisped.

The day Jenny set sail for China, she received a gift of £1000. "Thank you, Jesus, for this seal of approval," Hudson rejoiced.

In England, Hudson found

GUESS	1. the China Inland Mission was growing.
	2. missionaries were volunteering.
	3. the magazine was well known.

All those things were beyond anything Hudson had dreamed. Frequently he told missionary volunteers, "We do not have a penny for your passage to China." Time and time again the funds came in as needed. Hudson said good-bye to the new missionaries in London, and Jenny said hello to them in Shanghai.

In 1879, Hudson sailed for China himself. When he arrived in Shanghai, he

GUESS	1. was seriously ill.
	2. met Jenny.
	3. went to Chefoo.

Jenny met him in Shanghai and took her sick husband to Chefoo. The famine was over, and they talked far into the night about the orphan houses set up in North China, the needs of the children, and the mission stations.

This time the missionaries came from the stations to visit their leader. They prayed, rejoiced, and planned together in spite of Hudson's illness.

The missionaries had a problem. They had to decide whether or not

GUESS	1. to send their children to England.
	2. to keep their children on the mission field.
	3. to educate their children in China.

"We can't let them grow up not understanding the English language or customs," one mother said.

"My child acts more Chinese than English," another remarked.

"But if we send them so far away, we will not know them later. We have no part in their upbringing," another mother cried. "I do not want to part with my children!"

They

GUESS	1. prayed.
	2. thought of a plan.
	3. fasted.

Together they thought of a plan. Hudson agreed to set up a school for missionary children in Chefoo. He asked God for

GUESS	1. a principal.
	2. teachers.
	3. artists.

A year later the school was established with a principal and teachers.

15

China's Claims

By 1882 Hudson felt strong enough to attend a conference at Wuchang. Many missionaries who had worked since the founding of the mission in 1866 were

GUESS

1. quitting.
2. retiring.
3. dying.

After almost twenty years in China, many retired. That left the younger missionaries with more responsibility and duties. They wanted to talk to their leader, and they wondered about the future.

The famine had ended, but the orphans' homes were full of eager young children in need of care and food. Funds were low, and workers were few. Jenny Taylor lamented, "The future troubles never seem to run out."

Many of the new missionaries Hudson had interviewed in London were now in China; but Hudson had never visited them there. He wanted to share in their experiences and God's blessings.

They all decided to meet in Wuchang. This time Jenny stayed in London while Hudson made the trip. He wrote to her, "God is giving us a happy time of fellowship together."

At the convention, they decided to

GUESS	1. change the mission.
	2. ask for money.
	3. keep the same principles.

Hudson was happy the convention confirmed the same principles on which the society was founded. He said, "We must never do a *right* thing the *wrong* way."

The missionaries realized

GUESS	1. opportunities were open.
	2. inland Chinese wanted the gospel.
	3. there were not enough workers.

"Yes, we need to go into new lands," Wang-tsu agreed, "but we need more workers in the stations already established to the north, south, and west. Why open more stations when we can hardly operate the ones we have?"

"If we don't advance, we retreat!" Hudson replied. "Are we going to look at the difficulties or at God? Not to go forward is to throw away opportunities God has given. How long will these be open? Is it true, as the Chinese say, 'Even with our eyes open, we can't see Mount Tai'?"

The missionaries decided

GUESS	1. to pray for seventy new missionaries.
	2. to pray for thirty new missionaries.
	3. to pray for eighteen new missionaries.

They asked God for seventy new missionaries to come over a three-year period.

"Let us gather here again in three years to thank God for sending these missionaries to China," Mr. Rudland suggested.

"With all this work to do, we will be scattered all across China

106

in three years," Wang-tsu objected. "Why not thank Him now?"

"Before the seventy missionaries come?"

"Yes. We believe God will send them. Why not thank Him now?" Wang-tsu repeated.

"Why not?" Hudson beamed. "The more glorious the attempt, the more glorious the success!"

Holding hands, the entire group gathered around a map of China. Each one thanked God for giving seventy missionaries to the China Inland Mission.

Three years later

GUESS	1. seventy new missionaries were on the field. 2. thirty new missionaries were on the field. 3. eighteen new missionaries were on the field.

Seventy new missionaries went to China by 1884. Hudson wrote at that time, "I do feel more and more the blessedness of real trust in God."

One of the missionaries, John McCarthy, believed God wanted him to walk all the way across China from east to west, preaching the gospel as he went. Later, when Hudson went back to England, he took John with him.

Christian hearts stirred when Amelia's husband, Bay, arranged for John McCarthy, Dr. Soltan, and Mr. Stevenson to preach in the churches of England. People were eager to hear how the impossible had been brought to pass and how, without appeals for money or collections, the work grew.

A child in Cambridge wrote to Hudson Taylor, "If you are not dead yet, I want to send you the money I have saved up to help the little boys and girls of China to love Jesus."

Lord Radstock, who never forgot the China Inland Mission, wrote to Hudson,

GUESS	1. "You are a great help." 2. "You strengthen our faith." 3. "Ask for one hundred missionaries."

107

Lord Radstock sent a check for £500 and said, "Do not stop at seventy! Surely we shall see greater things than these if we seek God's glory."

Mr. Taylor published a new edition of his booklet *China's Spiritual Need and Claims*. He distributed this booklet when he spoke at Cambridge University. Seven of the best athletes at Cambridge offered themselves as missionaries to China.

Again and again their departure to China was delayed, though, because

> GUESS

1. they got sick.
2. they held revivals.
3. they were afraid to go.

Delays were caused by churches, who begged the Cambridge Seven to hold revival meetings. Christians in England loved the Cambridge Seven.

When they finally arrived in China, the Chinese also loved them. Many people believed because of the testimony of these seven athletes. "They are borne on a great wave of fervent enthusiasm!" Jenny Taylor exclaimed.

"CIM has become popular," Mr. Broomhall marveled. "Something we never expected or asked of God."

Again and again Hudson Taylor visited the missionaries in China. He went as often

> GUESS

1. as his health permitted.
2. as his work allowed.
3. as funds were available.

All those factors determined his trips to oversee the work on the field of inland China.

In 1887, at another conference, McCarthy and Stevenson suggested they ask for

1. thirty new workers.

| GUESS | 2. eighteen new workers.
| | 3. one hundred new workers.

They asked Hudson's permission to ask for one hundred. Hudson was speechless. *A hundred missionaries in one year!* He swallowed. No mission in existence had ever dreamed of sending out reinforcements on such a scale. "Lord Radstock suggested that before, but it seemed so impossible," Hudson remembered.

"Very well. One hundred. Only God can do the impossible," Hudson said.

In 1887, the number of missionaries who actually asked to go to China was

| GUESS | 1. one hundred.
| | 2. five hundred.
| | 3. six hundred.

Six hundred missionaries asked to go. One hundred two were chosen, equipped, and sent out. After all expenses were paid, $55,000 remained.

In 1888 Hudson Taylor was invited to America. He was received by D. L. Moody and the leaders of the Niagara Bible Conference. At that conference fourteen young men and women offered to become missionaries under the China Inland Mission, and the North American Council was formed.

The last twelve years of Hudson's life were years of worldwide ministry. The Scandinavians, Germans, Australians, and New Zealanders all welcomed him. All were impressed with a man almost sixty years old in such poor health, who bore tremendous burdens, yet remained absolutely calm and untroubled.

To all nationalities he said, "The China Inland Mission sprang from times of sickness and suffering on my part. Remember, it takes both rain and sunshine to make a rainbow! God put it into the hearts of men and women to do for Jesus what I could not do."

In 1902 Hudson passed the control of the mission to Mr. Hoste, saying, "Jesus does satisfy if we will let Him *be* all and *do* all." At that time CIM numbered seven hundred fifty missionaries.

On June 3, 1903, Hudson Taylor died beside the Chin-Kiang River in China. His life bore fruit as he bore the cross of suffering. Out of suffering came God's greatest warriors.

Moody Press, a ministry of the Moody Bible Institute, is designed for education, evangelization, and edification. If we may assist you in knowing more about Christ and the Christian life, please write us without obligation: Moody Press, c/o MLM, Chicago, Illinois 60610.